A Closer Talk with God

Scriptural Prayers for Women

Kim Trujillo

Scripture quotations are taken from the Holy Bible, New Living Translation, copyright ©1996, 2004, 2007 by Tyndale House Foundation. Used by permission of Tyndale House Publishers, Inc., Carol Stream, Illinois 60188. All rights reserved.

Scripture taken from the HOLY BIBLE, NEW INTERNATIONAL VERSION®. Copyright © 1973, 1978, 1984 Biblica. Used by permission of Zondervan. All rights reserved.

Scripture taken from *The Message*. Copyright © 1993, 1994, 1995, 1996, 2000, 2001, 2002. Used by permission of NavPress Publishing Group.

Scripture taken from the New King James Version®. Copyright © 1982 by Thomas Nelson, Inc. Used by permission. All rights reserved.

Scripture taken from GOD'S WORD®, © 1995 God's Word to the Nations. Used by permission of Baker Publishing Group.

Dedication

This book is dedicated to my mom, Priscilla Phelps, the one who encouraged me to go beyond being a reader to become a writer. I hope I've made you proud, Mama.

Table of Contents

Why Scriptural Prayer?

A better question might be: Why not? In Isaiah 55:8-11, we find the following verses: "For My thoughts are not your thoughts, neither are your ways My ways," declares the LORD. "As the heavens are higher than the earth, so are My ways higher than your ways and My thoughts than your thoughts. As the rain and the snow come down from heaven, and do not return to it without watering the earth and making it bud and flourish, so that it yields seed for the sower and bread for the eater, so is My word that goes out from My mouth. It will not return to Me empty, but will accomplish what I desire and achieve the purpose for which I sent it." (NIV)

These verses make it clear that there's no better way to pray than by praying God's own words back to Him, for His word cannot return to Him without results. His word always produces fruit in our lives and accomplishes whatever He desires. Knowing that His word will bring about godly results, why would we not take advantage of connecting to God in this way? Praying with scripture simply means a closer talk with God.

The Prayers

Creating prayers comprised only of scriptures is a lot of hard work. However, I have done the majority of the work for you. After narrowing down the number of topics that most women tend to pray about to twenty-two, I used various concordances and topical indexes to find relevant verses for each topic. I then organized the verses into prayers and wrote a personal introduction for each prayer. The prayers are organized chronologically by the times referred to in the introductions.

To make sure that they didn't sound like pieced-together prayers, I adjusted words here and there, but I kept the essential words and phrasing of the original verses from the Bible. Most of the verses came from the New Living Translation and the New International Version because they sound the most like how we speak today.

I purposely did not mark the prayers with footnotes or citations in order to make them easier to read. While reciting these prayers, you should be able to focus on what you say to God, not be distracted by references to book, chapter, and verse. For your benefit, though, you will find a list of all the verses used in each prayer at the end of the book.

Each prayer was written to be a stand-alone prayer. However, these prayers are not set in stone; they belong to you now. It is your choice how to use them. Once you choose one to pray, read through it closely and determine if it fits you and your situation. If it does, then you can say the prayer simply as it is written. If any part doesn't apply to you and your life, then delete the irrelevant lines. You may also find that the prayer is not personal enough; if so, revise the prayer to include your personal information. Make these prayers your own.

Although these prayers have been written specifically to be used by you, the reader, they also make good gifts for your family and friends who need a little encouragement in their prayers. Therefore, I give you my permission to share any of the prayers in this book with people you know.

I pray that you and those you know will be able to use these prayers to talk closer with God. I pray that you will see the value of praying from scripture and will begin to create your own scriptural prayers. And I pray God will bless you in all that you do.

Forgive My Sins

Sins, like fingerprints, are very personal things; no two people have the same list of sins. We may share some of the same sins, but what triggers them or how they manifest themselves in our lives differs. Although the Bible says that we are to confess our sins to one another, I'm not sure that means we should put them into print for the world to see. So, for now I will keep my list between God and me, and being the kind person that I am, I'll not ask you to share yours with me. Instead I'll encourage you to confess your sins to God, your Father, who understands your weaknesses, your temptations, and your evil desires. When you humbly admit them to Him, He will help break sin's control over you.

Forgive My Sins: Prayer

How can I know all the sins lurking in my heart? Cleanse me from these hidden faults. Keep me from deliberate sin! Don't let my evil desires control me. Then I will be free of guilt and innocent of great sin. May the words of my mouth and the thoughts of my heart be pleasing to You, O Lord, my rock and my redeemer. I will watch what I do and not sin in what I say; I will hold my tongue when the ungodly are around me. Don't let those who trust in You stumble because of me, and don't let me cause them to be humiliated.

Forgive the rebellious sins of my youth; look at me instead through the eyes of Your unfailing love, for You are merciful, O Lord. For the honor of Your name, forgive my many, many sins. O God, You know how foolish I am; my sins cannot be hidden from You. I do not understand what I do. For what I want to do I do not do, but what I hate to do, I do. It is not myself who does it, but it is the sin that is living in me. Have mercy on me; heal me, for I have sinned against You. When I refuse to confess my sin, I am weak and miserable, and I groan all day long. Day and night Your hand of discipline is heavy on me. If I confess all my sins to You and stop trying to hide them, if I say to myself, "I will confess my rebellion to the Lord," then You will forgive me! All my guilt will be gone. So search me, O God, and know my heart; test me and know my anxious thoughts. See if there is any offensive way in me, and lead me in the way everlasting.

You're the One I've violated, and You've seen it all, seen the full extent of my evil. You have all the facts before You; whatever You decide about me is fair. I've been out of step with You for a long time, in the wrong since before I was born. What You're after is the truth from the inside out. Going through the motions doesn't please You; a flawless performance is nothing to You. The sacrifice You want is a broken spirit, a broken and repentant heart. May my pain cause me to have remorse and change my ways. May You use the sorrow in my life to help me to turn away from sin and seek salvation.

Have mercy on me, O God, because of Your unfailing love. Because of Your great compassion, blot out the stain of my sins. Wash me clean from my guilt. Purify me from my sins, and I will be clean; wash me, and I will be whiter than snow. Though my sins are now like scarlet, they shall be as white as snow; though they are red like crimson, they shall be as wool.

Praise the Lord! For You have heard my cry for mercy. You are my strength, my shield from every danger. I trust in You with all my heart. You help me, and my heart is filled with joy. I burst out in songs of thanksgiving. Thank You for listening to my prayer. In Jesus' blessed name, I pray these things. Amen.

Salvation

The most important things you can do in your lifetime are give your life over to God, confess that Jesus Christ is your Lord and Savior, be baptized for the forgiveness of your sins and receive the Holy Spirit, then live the rest of your life as a new creature in God's grace. This prayer will remind you to be thankful for the free gift of salvation and will challenge you to live your life God's way.

Salvation: Prayer

Righteousness from God comes through faith in Jesus Christ to all who believe. All have sinned and fall short of the glory of God, but we are justified freely by His grace through the redemption that comes from Jesus Christ, through His death, burial, and resurrection. Salvation is found in no one else, no one but Jesus, for there is no other name under heaven given to men by which we must be saved.

I am so thankful that long ago, even before You made the world, You loved us and chose us in Christ to be holy and without fault in Your eyes. Your unchanging plan has always been to adopt us into Your own family by bringing us to Yourself through Jesus Christ.

I know I need to repent and be baptized in the name of Jesus Christ for the forgiveness of my sins, and I will receive the gift of the Holy Spirit. For those who are baptized into Christ Jesus are baptized into His death. Likewise, just as Christ was raised from the dead through the glory of the Father, they too may live a new life. So, what am I waiting for? I should get up, be baptized and wash my sins away, while calling on His name. I will repent and turn to You God, so that my sins may be wiped out, that times of refreshing may come from You Lord.

One day all of us will appear before the judgment seat of Christ, so that each of us may receive what is due him for the things done on this earth, whether good or bad things. Therefore, I make it my goal to please God. I am Your workmanship, created in Christ Jesus to do good works, which You prepared in advance for me to do. You began a good work in me and will carry it on until the day of Christ Jesus. I pray that with my unveiled face I will reflect the Lord's glory and be transformed into His likeness with ever-increasing glory.

Please help me not to go astray. Let me regularly examine myself to see whether I am still in the faith; let me test myself. I pray that I will love others more and more, that I will keep on growing in my knowledge and understanding. I pray that I will lead a pure and blameless life until Christ returns. May I live a life worthy of the Lord and may I please Him in every way: bearing fruit in every good work as I give thanks to the Father. It's in Jesus' name I pray. Amen.

Relieve My Fears

I guess I'm what you'd call a 'fraidy cat. I scare easily; just ask the policemen who had to come to our house two different times in the middle of night because I heard noises outside. I might mention though that those fearful moments were intensified because I was home alone with two small children since Johnny was working away from home at the time.

Fear has been no stranger to me. I've always been afraid of the dark. We had night lights in several rooms when I was a kid, and I've carried on the tradition as an adult. As a kid my family and I often went to the drive-in movie at Blytheville, and it seems like all of the movies back then were about giant animals like mice, rats, spiders, and snakes. I'd go home and have nightmares about these super-sized animals. Once as a teenager I read a couple of chapters of the book, Amityville Horror. I abandoned the book early because I was afraid to go to the bathroom by myself; I was scared there would be flies in the window and dark, scary stains in the toilet. My sister quickly tired of having to accompany me to the bathroom. (It's okay to laugh; I can laugh, too…now.)

Dying in a fire had never been a fear of mine until one fateful November night in 1979. My grandparents, M.S. and Alice Johnson, ran the Bronze Gate, a restaurant located on the first floor of the Chaffin Motor Hotel in Caruthersville, Missouri. We ate there several nights a week, but this night was different. As we waited for the food we'd ordered to be brought to our table, we heard lots of running and yelling coming from upstairs. Then we heard the cries of "Fire!" as smoke billowed down the stairs. We gathered our things as quickly as possible and headed outside away from the four-story building. The second and third floors were already ablaze. We helplessly watched as people jumped from the top floor. Fire departments from thirty miles away came to help put out the blaze, but to no avail. The building was destroyed, and three people weren't able to get out in time and lost their lives. As a result of this terrifying experience, I'm much more aware of the dangers of fire.

There are several fears that carried over from my childhood into my adult life. As a teen, I used to dream often of tornadoes. I vividly remember one dream in which a tornado wiped out my grandparents' red house on Carleton. In that dream, Caruthersville was like a dark war zone with fires blazing all over. Unfortunately, this fear basically came true on April 2, 2006 as a tornado destroyed about half of my hometown of Caruthersville. My parents were home at the time and took cover in the hallway as the tornado swept down the street behind their house. God spared them and every other person in town, but 600 residences were destroyed or damaged, including the home that I'd grown up in. From that day forward, my mom was terrified of storms.

That wasn't the only tornado that touched my life. On February 5, 2008, a tornado left a 123-mile path of destruction through Arkansas, and it came through Clinton right by the house we'd just vacated a few months before when we'd moved to Choctaw five miles away. We watched the tornado from our back door as it hit Clinton. This time there were two deaths, and several of our friends lost their homes and their businesses. Needless to say, I'm the one who nearly panics now when the weather calls start.

Fears are common; we all have them. Some of us (like me) just have more than others. But God is not a God of fear. The words, "Fear not," appear more than four hundred times in the Bible. God's word tells us not to fear earthquakes, bad news, authorities, insults, your enemies, and much, much more, but it also tells us that we should fear God, for He has the power to kill us and throw us into hell. Ecclesiastes 3:14 says that God's purpose is that people should fear Him.

In Isaiah 41, God says to fear not because He is the one who helps us. So, whenever fear enters your heart, remind yourself that God is the only one you should fear. He is more powerful than whatever is causing you to shake in your boots. He can calm you and alleviate your earthly fears, if you'll just let Him. Trust in His power, and above all, fear Him.

Relieve My Fears: Prayer

Good morning, Lord. Last night, I lay down and slept. This morning, I woke in safety, for You were watching over me. I delight in doing everything You want; day and night I think about Your law. I want to be like a tree planted along the riverbank, bearing fruit each season without fail. My leaves will never wither, and in all I do, I will prosper, for You watch over the path of the godly.

Bend down and listen to me; rescue me quickly from my fears. Be for me a great rock of safety, a fortress where my enemies (my fears) cannot reach me. As Your servant, I should fear not, for You are with me.

You tell me not to be afraid for You have ransomed me. You have called me by name; I am Yours. When I go through deep waters and great trouble, You will be with me. When I go through rivers of difficulty, I will not drown! When I walk through the fire of oppression, I will not be burned up; the flames will not consume me. For You are the Lord, my God, the Holy One of Israel, my Savior. I will not be afraid, for You are with me.

Even when I walk through the darkest valley, I will not be afraid, for You are close beside me. Your rod and Your staff protect and comfort me. I will wait patiently for the Lord. I will be brave and courageous. I will wait patiently for You.

I will not be afraid of the terrors of the night, nor fear the dangers of the day, nor dread the plague that stalks in darkness, nor the disaster that strikes at midday. For if I make the Lord my refuge, if I make the Most High my shelter, no evil will conquer me; no plague will come near my home. For You order Your angels to protect me wherever I go. You rescue those who love You. You protect those who trust in Your name. When I call on You, You will answer; You will be with me in trouble. You will rescue and honor me. You will satisfy me with a long life and give me Your salvation.

I will bless the Lord who guides me; even at night my heart instructs me. I know You are always with me. I will not be shaken, for You are right beside me. Tonight, I will lie down in peace and sleep, for you alone, O Lord, will keep me safe. Tomorrow I hope that I can say, "I prayed to the Lord, and He answered me, freeing me from all my fears. For the angel of the Lord guards all who fear Him, and He rescues them."

I am Your servant. I have been chosen to be known by You, and I understand that You alone are God. There is no other God; there never has been and never will be. You are the Lord, and there is no other Savior. I will not be afraid, for You will be with me and will take care of me. In Jesus' blessed and holy name, I pray. Amen.

Looking for a Spouse

Finding the right guy, the one that God wants you to spend the rest of your life with, is not easy. My hunt for the right man began when I was about twelve. I had crushes on several boys, a couple from school and one who was my mom's boss's son. I remember wishing for a boyfriend every time we crossed the bridge from Missouri to Tennessee or vice versa. Everyone knows that if you hold your breath the entire time you cross a bridge and make a wish, it will come true. There's no telling how many wishes I made before I realized that this was actually a myth.

I dated a couple of guys in high school, but it wasn't until my senior year that I really fell hard for a guy. Jimmy was three years younger than I was, and at first he kind of liked my sister who was closer to his age. When she didn't return his feelings, he started looking elsewhere and noticed me. We dated all of my senior year and off and on for the next four years.

He was my first love, and I dreamed of marrying him. However, he didn't feel the same way. He wasn't as sure about the longevity of our relationship. He wanted time to make sure I was the only one for him, so he spent a lot of time checking out the competition. He just wasn't ready to get married.

Finally during one of our off periods, I decided I had wasted enough of my life sitting around waiting on him and began dating again to see if maybe there was someone else out there for me, but no one seemed to last more than a couple of dates. Most of the guys I dated were immature and were not interested in marrying any time soon.

Then one night in March of 1993, I went with a friend for free line-dancing lessons at the Holiday Inn in Blytheville. There I met Johnny Trujillo, my Mr. Right. Johnny had been praying for a while that God would send him Mrs. Right, and God figured I was the right one for him. We knew right away that it was God's will that we met. For one, we lived four hours away from each other, so without God's help, we never would have found each other. I never dreamed that I would meet my future husband in a bar (and even though it happened for me, I wouldn't recommend it for you), but I did. We dated for two years and spent every weekend taking turns driving to each other's houses. Our love story ended in marriage when we eloped on July 3, 1995.

I pray that the following prayer will help you in your quest to find the love of your life and that you will be as happy in your marriage as I am in mine. I'd wish you luck, but I don't think luck plays any part in finding *your true love. It's all God's work. I pray that He will lead you directly to your knight in shining armor.*

Looking for a Spouse: Prayer

With all my heart I will praise you, O Lord my God. I will give glory to Your name forever. My heart is confident in You, O God; no wonder I can sing Your praises! Your goodness is so great! You place Your hand of blessing on my head.

Create in me a clean heart, O God. Renew a right spirit within me. Teach me Your ways, O Lord, that I may live according to Your truth! Grant me purity of heart, that I may honor You.

You know Lord how much I long for a Christian husband who will love me as I am. My heart has been broken. Depression haunts my days. My groans come from an anguished heart. Answer me when I call, O God who declares me innocent. Take away my distress. Have mercy on me and hear my prayer.

When I am around men, help me to remember that my body is not meant for sexual immorality, but for the Lord, and the Lord for my body. Let there not be even a hint of sexual immorality, or of any kind of impurity, or of greed, because these are improper for God's holy people.

While I am single, I will remember that an unmarried woman is concerned about the Lord's affairs; her aim is to be devoted to the Lord in both body and spirit. But a married woman is concerned about the affairs of this world--how she can please her husband. For now let me be devoted to the apostles' teaching and to fellowship, to the breaking of bread and to prayer.

I so want to be able to tell people that I asked You to give me a lifelong mate and You have given me my request. You have heard my plea; You have answered my prayer. I will praise You forever, O God, for what You have done. I keep right on praying to You, Lord, hoping this is the time You will show me favor. In your unfailing love, O God, answer my prayer.

I pray that my future husband and I will clothe ourselves with compassion, kindness, humility, gentleness, and patience. We will bear with each other and forgive whatever grievances we will have against each other. Please let the peace of Christ rule in our hearts.

Patience is not easy. Help me to be still in Your presence and wait patiently for You to act. Help me not to worry about those who prosper and have the things I want. Instead, I will wait for Your mercies. I know You have plans for me, plans to give me hope and a future. As I wait, I pray that I will live a life worthy of the calling I have received. In Jesus' blessed name, I pray these things. Amen.

To Be a Better Wife

There was nothing hard about getting married; I loved Johnny and knew I wanted to live the rest of my life as his wife. But moving four hours away from home and being alone three nights a week was a hard adjustment for me. Then add two small children, a new job, and no friends to the mix, and I was not a happy camper during those first few years of our marriage. Poor Johnny. He'd come home from work on Thursdays expecting to be king of his castle, and I'd meet him at the door with my list of expectations. Need I say that mine in no way resembled his? There was definitely trouble in paradise.

Thank God, though, that we weren't the only ones experiencing marriage pains. Our congregation offered a His Needs, Her Needs class on Sunday nights for a couple of months early on in our marriage. We attended along with about five other couples whose marriages also weren't going as planned. Through the class and the readings for the class, we began communicating better about our wants, desires, likes, dislikes, etc. This class forced us to talk about all those things that we should have been talking about in the first place. Instead we had allowed them to become topics for arguments.

That class, along with prayer and God's assistance, saved our marriage. We learned so much and believed so strongly in the techniques taught in the class, that we attended it the next two times it was offered at our church, too. I would recommend this class to anyone who wants to better their marriage. A shared love for the Lord is the foundation to a good marriage, but communication follows closely behind.

In the class, we learned about the Love Bank concept and how each person has his/her own bank. Our spouses make deposits into our bank when they respect us, admire us, spend time with us, etc. They make withdrawals when they hurt us, anger us, neglect us, etc. The following prayer is based on this concept. It's all about making deposits into your husband's bank, with the help of the Lord, of course. If you want to be a better wife to your husband, the following prayer should help.

To Be a Better Wife: Prayer

You have said You will answer when I call to You. Have mercy on me today and hear my prayer about my marriage.

Let my husband and me be quick to listen, slow to speak, and slow to get angry. Help us not to sin by ever letting anger gain control over us. Let us think about whatever troubles us overnight and remain silent. Remind us that anger can never make things right in Your sight.

I pray, Lord, that as husband and wife, we will share each other's troubles and problems. Let us learn the secret of being content in any and every situation, whether well fed or hungry, whether living in plenty or in want. Let us remember that we can do everything through Him who gives us strength.

Your Word states that as a wife, I should be submissive to my husband. If I need to be submissive to his will in any area, then I pray that You will give me peace over it.

When it comes to the marital bed, help me to remember that by being his wife, I have given him authority over my body. I will not deprive him of sexual relations, and I will not lust after other men. I am my husband's, and he is mine. Let our love flash like fire, the brightest kind of flame. Let him be content with me as his lover. Help me to be a good wife to my husband, responsive to his needs. May our love be better than wine. Make us dear, dear friends, as well as lovers.

Let him think me lovely and beautiful and call me his beloved. Help me remember that what matters is not my outward appearance – the styling of my hair, the jewelry I wear, the cut of my clothes – but my inner disposition. Cultivate my inner beauty, the beauty that comes from within, the unfading beauty of a gentle and quiet spirit, which is so precious to You God.

Love cannot be bought or sold; it can't be found in the marketplace. I want to love him with sincere love. I want to be patient and kind, not jealous, boastful, proud, or rude. I do not want to be irritable or keep a record of his wrongs. Let us never give up on each other.

Help my husband have full confidence in me and my opinions, and help me to greatly enrich his life. In the same way, may my husband give honor to me and treat me with understanding as we live together. In some ways, I am weaker than him, but I am his equal partner in Your gift of new life. Allow him to treat me as he should, so his prayers will be heard.

You will work out everything in our lives to its proper end. Help me to trust You in all matters, no matter what the result may be. Let me not worry about my life, but let us commit to You, Lord, whatever we do, and You will establish Your plans. May You give us the desires of our hearts and make all of our plans succeed. Find a way that both of us will be content and we can provide well for our family. May our beginnings seem humble, for so prosperous will our future be because we trust in You. Help us to trust in You, Lord. Help us to know which path each day to take.

As a couple, let us draw close to You. Let us purify our hearts and bow down before You. We will admit our dependence on You, and You will draw close to us. Let the smile of Your face shine on us, Lord. In Your Son Jesus' name I pray. Amen.

We Want a Baby

This prayer was originally written a few years ago specifically for a newly married young couple at our church. Like many newlyweds, they felt a baby would be the perfect addition to their new family unit. Unfortunately, getting pregnant wasn't happening as fast as they wished, and they wondered why God wasn't blessing them yet with a child. With tears in her eyes, this young wife mentioned several times in ladies' class how desperate she was for a baby of her own. I wrote this prayer for her.

If you are trying to get pregnant, remember you are not alone; there are thousands of women out there who suffer the same monthly disappointment as you do. And remember you are not the first person who has had to wait for a child; the Bible is full of stories of women who cried out to the Lord for a child of their own. Don't become so wrapped up in this desire, though, that you miss out on the blessings that God is sending you each day while you wait. Be patient. As the old saying goes, it will probably happen when you least expect it. But if it's meant to happen, it will be in God's time on God's terms.

We Want a Baby: Prayer

Heavenly Father, I pray from Your Word today. Listen to my voice this morning, Lord. Each morning I bring my requests to You and wait expectantly. God, hear Your servant's prayer! Listen as I plead.

With all my heart I will praise you, O Lord my God. I will give glory to Your name forever. My heart is confident in You, O God; no wonder I can sing your praises! Your goodness is so great! You have stored up great blessings for those who honor You. You have done so much for those who come to You for protection, blessing them before the watching world. You both precede and follow me. You place Your hand of blessing on my head.

You know Lord how busy I have been lately and how my husband and I have been praying for a baby. I am exhausted, and now my heart is broken. Depression haunts my days; my groans come from an anguished heart. Answer me when I call, O God. Take away my distress. Have mercy on me and hear my prayer.

In Your Word, You have declared that as my God You will prosper me abundantly in all the work of my hand, in the offspring of my body, for You will again rejoice over me for good, just as You rejoiced over my father and grandfathers. With all my heart I want Your blessings. Be merciful just as You promised. May You grant my heart's desire and fulfill all our plans. Help me to take delight in You Lord, and You will give me my heart's desires. With all my heart I want Your blessings. Be merciful just as You promised.

Children are a blessing, and we want a child so badly. Children are a gift and a reward from You. I so want to be able to tell people that I asked the Lord to give me this child, and He has given me my request. The Lord has heard my plea; the Lord has answered my prayer. I will praise You forever, O God, for what You have done. I keep right on praying to You, Lord, hoping this is the time You will show me favor. Bend down, O Lord, and hear my prayer; answer me, for I need your help. Answer me because You are faithful and righteous.

Patience is not easy. Help me to be still in the presence of You Lord and wait patiently for You to act. Help me not to worry about people who prosper and have the things I want. Instead, I will wait quietly before God, for my hope is in Him. For I know that You still wait for me to come to You so You can show me Your love and compassion. For the Lord is a faithful God. Blessed are those who wait for Him to help them.

But these things I plan won't happen right away. Slowly, steadily, surely, the time approaches when the vision will be fulfilled. If it seems slow, I will wait patiently, for it will surely take place. It will not be delayed. But if we look forward to something we don't have yet, we must wait patiently and confidently. For we who live by the Spirit eagerly wait to receive everything promised to us who are right with God through faith. In Jesus' blessed name, I pray these things. Amen.

During Pregnancy

Even though I've only been pregnant twice, I have learned what most women will tell you: no two pregnancies are exactly alike. Take my two, for instance. There were a couple of similarities, of course. For instance, I didn't have any morning sickness either time, which was definitely a blessing. However, I was so sleepy in the evenings, almost comatose at times. I would be asleep on the couch by 6:00 each night for the first three or four months of the pregnancy. That was fine with the first pregnancy as I was home alone most of the time, but it was a little harder with the second considering I had a fourteen month old whose bedtime wasn't until 8:00. As you know, toddlers can get into a lot of mischief in two hours when no one is watching.

My food cravings were different with each pregnancy. I craved salty foods with Brandon, my first child. Cheetos were my best friend. I even kept a bag at school for my afternoon snack between classes. With Savanah, I craved ice cream. Sonic made a killing off of me those nine months. I graced their establishment every afternoon for an ice cream cone or sundae, and some days I went twice. What's especially weird is that my kids tend to gravitate toward the same foods today that I craved while pregnant with them. Brandon is into the salty foods like chips and dip, processed meats, and for ten years Cheetos were his favorite food. Savanah, on the other hand, craves sweets. Her dad fusses about how much sugar she puts in her coffee, and pre-sweetened cereals apparently aren't sweet enough for her since she sometimes adds a squirt of honey to each bite of Cheerios.

With Brandon I had so much energy, but not so much with Savanah. When I was nine months pregnant with Brandon, I climbed Sugar Loaf Mountain on Greers Ferry Lake, which if you knew me, you'd know what a big deal that was. And a week before he was born, I attended the annual Chuck Wagon Races on Labor Day weekend. The heat was killer, and I'm sure that to get to our seats we had to walk down the side of a cliff. With Savanah, I don't remember doing anything that required much energy, but then again I had a toddler to take care of, so I probably used up all of my energy keeping up with him.

I can honestly say I loved being pregnant. I got lots of positive attention from everyone, my students were so sweet to me and gave me baby showers for both of my children, and I wasn't sick even one time.

But I know that not all women are blessed with healthy or easy pregnancies. Lots of women deal with extreme morning sickness. Many face bad news from their doctors about the health of their unborn babies.

And others suffer through the death of their little ones, either through miscarriage or stillborn births. This prayer is for all pregnant women, but especially for those with more difficult pregnancies who worry about their unborn child and themselves.

During Pregnancy: Prayer

Heavenly Father, You say that Your Word is living and active, that it is sharper than any double-edged sword. It penetrates even to dividing soul and spirit, joints and marrow. Therefore, Lord, I will pray from Your Word today.

I rise this day and cry for help; I have put my hope in Your word. I will meditate on Your promises. To You I call, O Lord my Rock; do not turn a deaf ear to me. Hear my cry for mercy as I call to You for help. Come quickly to help me, O Lord my Savior. Let the Word of the Lord now be fulfilled!

As Hannah prayed in her heart for the gift of a baby, so I also have prayed. You heard that prayer and answered it with the blessing of this child that is forming inside of me. This child is a gift from You Lord, a reward from You.

You created this baby's inmost being; You knit this child together in my womb. I praise You because this baby is fearfully and wonderfully made; Your works are wonderful, I know that full well. My baby's frame was not hidden from You when made in the secret place. When this baby was woven together in the depths of the earth, Your eyes saw my child's unformed body. All the days ordained for this child were written in Your book before one of them came to be.

I am amazed at the mysterious way this tiny baby is being formed in my womb. However, like Hannah, I am a woman who is deeply troubled, and I am pouring out my soul to You, Lord. I am worried. I pray that You will hear my prayer like You heard Hannah's and that my child will arrive healthy like hers. I pray You will give me peace and grant me what I ask of You this day. I ask that as Your servant, I find favor in Your eyes and that I will be able to go on my way, eat something, and that my face will no longer be downcast.

Like the woman who touched the hem of Jesus' robe, I come trembling and fall to Your feet. I pray that You will notice me and hear my prayer. I pray that Jesus will say to me, "Daughter, your faith has healed you. Go in peace."

Be merciful to me, Lord, for I am faint; heal me, for my body is in agony, and my soul is in anguish. Turn Your ear to me; answer quickly; deliver me. I am worn out from groaning; bring health to my body and nourishment to my bones. May You richly bless this child within me.

To You, O Lord, I call; to You I cry for mercy. Hear and be merciful to my child and me; be my help. Turn my wailing into dancing; remove my sackcloth and clothe me with joy, that my heart may sing to You and not be silent. O Lord my God, I will give you thanks forever. In Jesus' holy name, I pray these things. Amen.

For a Working Mother

I don't know about you, but I'm a full-time wife, a full-time mom, and a full-time employee, and there are many times where the three overlap. In order to make it through most days, I have to stop and pray to God – for energy, for strength, for wisdom, and yes, even for patience. God put me in each of these roles, so there's nothing wrong with asking Him for help when I feel like I'm failing to measure up to what He wants me to be.

This prayer was originally written several years ago for a friend of mine. At the time, she had a job she loved, a supportive husband, and children she adored. However, like most moms, she suffered from the I-feel-like-I-have-to-do-it-all-by-myself syndrome and felt that she was struggling to juggle all the aspects of her life. She called me her prayer warrior (which is an intimidating label) and asked me to pray, which I did. I went a step further, though, and wrote this prayer for her, too.

Much of the following prayer comes from Proverbs 31, which focuses on "A Wife of Noble Character." This idealized woman has it all: a husband who respects and praises her, children who love and obey her, and several jobs that keep her busy from sunup to after sundown. She is energetic, strong, industrious, generous, brave, wise, and kind, just to name a few. She manages her time well and works from home, and even though she has servants, she still feels compelled to fix meals for her family herself. She dresses well and accompanies her husband to community events. She does charity work and is held in high esteem by everyone who knows her.

Solomon says that she is praised greatly because she fears the LORD. Maybe we need to learn from her example. We should fear the LORD and take all of our jobs seriously. As Paul tells the Colossians, whatever we do, we should work at it with all of our hearts, as working for the Lord, not human masters (Col. 3:23). This applies to us working moms as well. We should put our whole hearts into our jobs whether we're at home or on the work front. Picture Jesus signing your paychecks, and above all else, pray.

For a Working Mother: Prayer

I praise Your name, for it is good. Hear me as I pray; consider my sighing. Listen to my cry for help, my King and my God, for I will never pray to anyone but You. In the morning, O Lord, You hear my voice; in the morning I lay my requests before You and wait in expectation. I come to You, weary and burdened, and know that You will give me rest.

Lead me, in Your righteousness; make straight Your way before me. I love You, Lord, and I want to serve You with all my heart and soul. Lord, bless me as I fear You, as I walk in Your ways. How great is the love You have lavished on me, that I should be called a child of God. Lord, give me strength and bless me with Your peace. I delight in You, Lord. Give me the desires of my heart.

Though I feel like I am stumbling right now, I will not be afraid, for You are with me. I will not be dismayed because You are my God, and You will strengthen me and help me. You will uphold me with Your hand and make my steps firm. I want again to walk in fellowship with You, Father, and with Your son Jesus Christ. Help me to set my mind on things above, not on earthly things, for Your way is perfect.

You, O Lord, keep my lamp burning at work; You turn my darkness there into light. With Your help I can advance; with You, I can scale this wall. You can deliver me from all my troubles. Lord, let me eat the fruit of my labor for You say blessings and prosperity will be mine. Like Solomon, I realize that it is good and proper to find satisfaction in my toilsome labor for this is my lot. Moreover, when You give me wealth, possessions, and good health, and allow me to enjoy them and be happy in my work, I will acknowledge these things as gifts from You. I rarely look back with sorrow on the past, for You have given me reasons for joy. I look forward to the day when I can say that You have delivered me from all of my troubles at work.

Help me to be a wife and mother of noble character. Let my husband have full confidence in me. Let me bring him good, not harm, all the days of my life. Let me work with eager hands. I want to set about my work vigorously. Let our family be able to open our arms to the poor and extend our hands to the needy. Let my husband be respected in the community and in our congregation. Clothe me with strength and dignity so I can laugh at the days to come. Let me speak with wisdom and faithful instruction to my children. I want to watch over the affairs of my household and not be idle. Let me fix these words of Yours in my heart and mind; let me teach them to my children, talking about them when we sit at home and when we travel in the car, when we lie down and when we get up. Let my children call me blessed; may my husband also, and may he praise me. As a wife and mother, I want to be like a fruitful vine within my house. Let my works at home bring You praise.

No matter what is going on in my life, Lord, let me be joyful always, pray continually, and give thanks in all circumstances, for this is Your will. May my whole spirit, soul, and body be blameless at the coming of our Lord Jesus Christ. In His blessed name, amen.

Safety

I don't know why, but I've always had this irrational fear that I'll die in a car wreck. When I lived in Caruthersville, it was highly unlikely that I'd die in a wreck considering the speed limit there was 25 mph and there were dips at almost every intersection. However, when I began dating Johnny, I spent sixteen hours a month traveling the busy highways of rural Arkansas where I envisioned being smushed in a head-on collision with a Wal-Mart semi or running into a ditch as I avoided a run-in with a crazy deer. Now, I live in Clinton, a small town in central Arkansas, which averages about one car-related fatality a month. So now I feel that my fear is a little more reasonable.

We all know that we really don't have much control over what happens on the road. That's why I have to talk to God so much while I'm driving. I feel the need to pray that there won't be any deer who cross my path, that there will be an opening in traffic so I can make a left-hand turn, that the other drivers will stay in their lanes and not mine, and that I won't be pulled over by a cop (although it's highly unlikely since I refuse to drive more than two miles over the speed limit). I also thank God continuously while on the road...for little things like the light changing to green to the big things like surviving the near head-on collision on the highway. Safety in the car is a big deal to me, so it ranks high on my prayer list.

The only other time I remember worrying about my safety is when I had to have a hysterectomy back in 1999. Having a couple of weeks till the surgery, I began picturing all of the things that could go wrong during surgery. I just knew that I was going to die while I was under anesthesia, and I worried about how Johnny was going to take care of two kids under the age of three without me. Needless to say, a few days before the surgery, I was stressed to the max. I confessed my fears in our couples' Sunday school class, so Dewey had us all stand and hold hands while he prayed for me and my upcoming surgery. Immediately, this unbelievable peace flowed through my body, and I was no longer afraid. I quit worrying and was able to put my complete trust in God.

So, let me just remind you: Our Father, God in heaven, is both omniscient and omnipotent; He loves us abundantly; and He is the only one who can provide us with all the protection we need. So, the next time you are worried about your safety, whether it's while you're driving down a busy highway, preparing for surgery, getting on a plane, walking down a dark alley, or just sitting in your living room, take a moment to talk to God, and ask Him for His all-powerful protection and His peace.

Safety: Prayer

Your word says that whoever trusts in You will be kept safe. So I pray, keep me safe, O God, for in You I take refuge. You are a shield to all who come to You for protection. I trust in You with all my heart. Direct my paths, O Lord. How great is the goodness You have stored up for those who fear You. You lavish it on those who come to You for protection, blessing them before the watching world. May Your angel set up a circle of protection around me while I pray.

Provide us a shelter and shade from the heat of the day and a refuge and hiding place from the storm and rain. You are my guardian; right at my side to protect me. You shield me from sunstroke, shelter me from moonstroke. You guard me from every evil; You guard my very life. You guard me when I leave and when I return; You guard me now; You guard me always. You see me when I travel and when I rest at home. You know everything I do. O Lord, if it is true that I have found favor with You, then please travel with us. We humble ourselves before You God and ask You for a safe journey. Just like You went ahead of the Israelites in a pillar of cloud or a pillar of fire, go ahead of us and allow us safe travel. O Lord, keep us safe and protect us.

Keep me from the hands of the wicked; protect me from men of violence. You are my hiding place; You will protect me from trouble and surround me with songs of deliverance. Order Your angels to protect me wherever I go. You have given me the shield of your salvation. Your right hand supports me. Your gentleness makes me great. You are my bodyguard, shielding every bone, so not even a finger gets broken.

You are a solid rock under my feet, breathing room for my soul, an impregnable castle. I'm set for life. You are granite strength and are a safe harbor. I trust You absolutely; You are a safe place to be. Rescue me from hidden traps; shield me from deadly hazards; Your arms fend off all harm. No harm will graze me; I will stand untouched; for You are my refuge.

You are my Father; You love me and keep me safe in the care of Jesus Christ. As Your child, I live in a peaceful place, in a safe home, and have quiet places of rest. I will lie down and sleep in peace, for You alone, O Lord, keep me safe. The spacious, free life is from You; it's also protected and safe. God-strengthened, I will be delivered from evil. When I run to You, You will rescue me from every evil attack and will bring me safely to Your heavenly kingdom. To You be glory for ever and ever. In Jesus' name. Amen.

Daily Worries

God does listen to us, and He does care about us, every minute of every day. Therefore, to God there is nothing too small to offer up to him in prayer. When my children were young, they reminded me of this constantly.

One incident especially stands out in my mind. Brandon was about three, which means Savanah was only one. A couple from church, Larry and Sonja, were babysitting them while Johnny and I were away on a date. For some reason, Sonja had to take the kids somewhere in their car. She had Brandon get in first and buckled him into his booster seat, but when she went to buckle Savanah's car seat in, she just could not get the seatbelt to fasten. She took the car seat out two or three times, perplexed about why the seatbelt wouldn't function. With the faith of a child, Brandon said, "We need to pray about it," and so they did. Of course, God answered my boy's prayer immediately. The next time she tried the seatbelt, it clicked right into place. Knowing my son, I'm sure he then said something like, "See, I told you; we just needed to pray."

Whether we're praying for large worries like sick loved ones, financial troubles, and addictions or we're praying for the small, everyday worries like seatbelts that need fastening, a safe left turn in traffic, and missing keys, we can trust God in all things. God is my Father, and I don't want to limit my conversations with Him only to the huge events in my life. He's my Daddy, and I can tell him anything. God wants us to feel comfortable talking to Him about every aspect of our lives, including our day-to-day worries. So go to Him for the small things, but even then, do so with a humble attitude, recognizing your total dependence on Him.

Daily Worries: Prayer

I come to You in prayer, using the powerful words You have given us in Your Bible, for the Word of God is living and active. Sharper than any double-edged sword, it penetrates even to dividing soul and spirit, joints and marrow.

My soul finds rest in You alone; my salvation comes from You. You alone are my rock and my salvation; You are my fortress, I will never be shaken. I will trust in You at all times, pouring out my heart to You, for You are my refuge. You are strong, and You are loving, O Lord.

You declare, "I know the plans I have for you, plans to prosper you and not to harm you, plans to give you hope and a future." Help me to trust You and Your plans for our lives.

My ambition is to lead a quiet life, to mind my own business and to work with my hands. I pray that I am content with what I have, for I have enough food and clothing. I pray that I am not like people who long to be rich and fall into temptation and are trapped by many foolish and harmful desires that plunge them into ruin and destruction. I know that the love of money is at the root of all kinds of evil and that many people, craving money, have wandered from the faith and pierced themselves with many sorrows. I pray that my desires are neither foolish nor harmful and that I will not fall into ruin or destruction or wander from my faith.

You say for us not to worry about anything; instead to pray about everything. So God, I am here telling You what I need and thanking You for all that You have done in my life. I want to experience Your peace which is far more wonderful than the human mind can even understand. I pray that Your peace will guard my heart and my mind as I live in Christ Jesus. Help me not to conform to the pattern of this world, but be transformed by the renewing of my mind. Then I will be able to test and approve what Your will is--Your good, pleasing and perfect will. I pray that whatever I do, whether in word or deed, let me do it all in the name of the Lord Jesus, giving thanks to You, Father, through Him.

I know there are people who say, "Today or tomorrow we are going to a certain town and will stay there a year. We will do business there and make a profit." Yet how do they know what will happen tomorrow? Our lives are like the morning fog – here a little while, then gone. What those people should say is, "If the Lord wants us to, we will live and do this or that." Otherwise, they will be boasting about their own plans, and all such boasting is evil. I pray that I will not be like those people boasting of future plans. I pray that I will not worry about tomorrow, for tomorrow will worry about itself. Each day has enough trouble of its own, and I pray for deliverance from my current troubles. I need to be careful how I live, not as a fool but as one who is wise.

Help me to remember that You are my shepherd; I have everything I need. You let me rest in green meadows; You lead me beside peaceful streams. You renew my strength. You guide me along right paths, bringing honor to Your name. You prepare a feast for me in the presence of my enemies. You welcome me as a guest, anointing my head with oil. My cup overflows with blessings. Surely Your goodness and unfailing love will pursue me all the days of my life, and I will live in the house of the Lord forever. Through Jesus' name I pray. Amen.

Friendship

Making friends has never been easy for me. Being painfully shy as a child and always having a book in my face didn't help matters any. Plus I had my sister Kellie to hang out with, so I didn't really need any friends early on. Then in high school, I met Tonya who shared some of the same interests as me: band, reading, and a guy named Robert. Tonya, whose nickname was "Bum," (don't criticize, it was the '80's) and I spent a lot of time writing notes to each other, calling one another on the phone, and riding around "the loop." We stayed close throughout high school, but drifted apart when I went to college.

Two years after college, I married Johnny and moved two hundred miles from home to live in Clinton, Arkansas, and realized how lonely I really was. In my mind, I pictured becoming close friends with one of the teachers from school who was close to my age. Although I hung out sporadically with a couple of teachers from school, we just didn't have enough in common to become besties.

For about five years, I whined and cried weekly to my poor, dear husband about my lack of a best friend and kind of looked to him to fulfill that role, which really was impossible if you think about it. One of the main jobs of a best friend is to be a listener to all the problems going on in the best friend's life. Well, the only problems I had at that time usually involved a difference in opinion with my husband, and I couldn't exactly spill my guts to him and expect any sympathy, now could I?

Fortunately, Johnny's prayer life at the time was stronger than mine. He must have prayed every day for me to find a friend. Finally, around 2000 God answered his prayer and sent the perfect best friend for me: Tammy Sykes, my niece by marriage. Being related and close in age is what originally drew us together; we attended the same church and ended up staying after church services and talking about family issues (seeing how life around here tends to run like a soap opera).

Having children about the same age also allowed us to bond. She has a son and daughter, too, who are two years older than my kids, which made them perfect playmates over the years. Because her kids were older than mine, I would seek Tammy's advice whenever my kids would go through difficult stages because I knew that she had already survived those stages. I would encourage her as she experienced those stages with her kids first, and she would reassure me when I later went through the same things with my kids.

Tammy is truly my best friend. We think so much alike that it's scary sometimes. We support one another during difficult times with our marriages and share advice and stories about raising our kids. Tammy and I talk for hours on the phone or sometimes we just send one-liners through texts that only we would understand. We share a love of books, and we've shared the job of teaching our ladies' class at church for the past few years. Some days I feel closer to her than anyone else on this earth. She's always encouraging me with sweet notes or ten-page letters or surprising me with little gifts, like teddy bears or pictures of fairies she's drawn just for me. She trusts me with her secrets and shares her troubles, her fears, and her sorrows with me, and I do the same with her. If we go too long without hanging out, we get "withdrawals" and have to have Tammy time, as I call it. (She probably calls it Kim time or something equally lame). We are closer than sisters, and I thank God constantly for bringing her into my life.

The Bible mentions friends in several places. Abraham was God's friend, and the Bible says that God spoke to Moses face to face as though He were speaking to a friend. David and Jonathan met and immediately became friends with a bond of love between them. People claimed Jesus was friends with tax collectors and sinners, and He Himself called several people His friends, including Lazarus and the unnamed man on the mat that was lowered through the roof. Jesus even acknowledged Judas Iscariot as His "friend" when he turned Jesus over to the men who had come to arrest him.

Seeing all of these examples of friendships in the Bible re-emphasizes to me the importance of godly friendships in this life. He sends people into our lives that we sometimes don't expect or realize we need. They build us up, encourage us, listen to us, admonish us, and help to carry our burdens. God wants us to pray for those we love, including our friends. So, this letter is dedicated to those friendships.

Friendship: Prayer

I devote myself to this prayer with an alert mind and a thankful heart. I can never stop thanking You for all the generous gifts You have given me, now that I belong to Christ Jesus. You keep me strong and free from all blame. You invited me into this wonderful friendship with Your Son, Jesus Christ our Lord.

I ask You to make me wise with spiritual wisdom so the way I live will always honor and please You, and I will continually do good, kind things for others. And all the while, I will learn to know You better and better.

When it comes to my friends, clothe me with compassion, kindness, humility, gentleness, and patience. Help us to carry each other's loads without comparing ourselves to one another. Help us not to be jealous, proud, rude, or irritable, and let us keep no records of wrongs. Let us make allowance for each other's faults and be forgiving when we offend one another.

Let love bond us together in perfect harmony, and let the peace that comes from Christ rule in our hearts. I pray we never grow weary in doing good for each other. Let us find time to meet together so we can encourage one another and build each other up. I don't want to love my friends with just words, but also with actions and truth.

Help me to get rid of the log in my own eye before I try to help my friend deal with the speck in her eye. Let me do for my friends as I'd have them do for me. Please do not let my close friends, those whom I trust, please do not let them turn against me. As friends we should love each other at all times, so let us be closer than brothers and sisters and be there for each other in times of adversity.

Make it possible for us to lead blameless lives, to do what is right, to speak the truth from sincere hearts, and to refuse to slander, harm, or speak evil of each other. Let us give each other good advice and never lead each other astray. Encourage us to confess our sins to one another and to pray for one another so we will be whole and healed. Above all, let us love one another as You love us. In Jesus' holy name, I pray these things. Amen.

Let Me Forgive

For the most part, I don't have trouble with forgiving others. One time, our preacher did a sermon on how dangerous an unforgiving heart can be. At the end of his sermon, he had members of the congregation come to the front to grab a rock from the buckets on the stage to represent each person in their lives that they had not yet forgiven. I had no need to go forward because I had no hard feelings toward anyone.

I do tend to get angry easily (probably because I am super sensitive), but I also forgive quickly. I don't like having ill feelings toward others, but there were two times in my life that I remember doing so. Once was toward a lady from church who had claimed that in Sunday school our son was becoming "a thorn in her side." As his mother, that just didn't set right by me. However, after being upset for a week or so, I talked with her, and we worked things out. We were able to move on like those words had never happened. The other incident was more serious. Several years ago while on vacation, I offended someone who misunderstood something I said to her grandchild. She went into protective grandma-bear mode and reacted by saying some hurtful things about me. Having not had the opportunity to speak to her since then, I don't know if she is still angry with me or not, but I do know that not much later I forgave her and put the matter behind me.

I'm not sure what kind of person you are, whether you forgive easily or hold grudges. But I do know that if you do not forgive those who hurt you, that you do not hurt them; you hurt yourself. God feels strongly about forgiveness. He even says that if we do not forgive others, that He will not forgive us. That's a good enough reason right there to forgive everyone who is on your unforgiven list. Maybe the following prayer will help to heal your broken heart.

Let Me Forgive: Prayer

I am confident that Your word, when You send it out, always produces fruit. It will accomplish all that You want it to, and it will prosper everywhere You send it. With this in mind, enable me to speak Your word with boldness.

Let me not copy the behavior and customs of this world, but transform me into a new person by changing the way I think, for Your will is good and pleasing and perfect. Because of Your love, I want always to be humble and gentle, patient with others, making allowance for their faults. Let me remember that You forgave me, so I must forgive others. Give me wisdom and patience, for it is to Your glory for me to overlook offenses. Because I am one of Your chosen people, clothe me with compassion, kindness, humility, gentleness, and patience. Help me to get rid of all anger, rage, and malice.

LORD, Your word says not to hold anything against anyone, to forgive him so that You will forgive me. Repeatedly, You say that if I forgive others who sin against me, You will forgive my sins against You. Jesus told Peter that he was to forgive his brother up to seventy times seven. Let me be as merciful as that.

Whenever I am angry, do not let me sin. Let me forgive quickly, and do not let the sun go down on my anger. I know an angry person starts fights and a hot-tempered person commits all kinds of sin. Let me not be that type of person. Likewise, help me not make friends with angry or hot-tempered people, or I may learn to be like them.

I almost feel like the one who has hurt me is my enemy at this time. Instead of taking revenge, which I feel like doing, let me remember that Your word says that I am instead to feed him and give him drink, and in this way heap burning coals of shame on his head. Let me be reconciled to my brother or sister before I next go before Your altar.

Test me, O LORD, examine my mind and heart, for Your love is ever before me, and I walk continually in Your truth. Teach my Your way, O LORD, and I will walk in Your truth; give me an undivided and forgiving heart, that I may honor You. Let me live a life filled with love for others, following the example of Christ, who loves me and gave Himself as a sacrifice to take away my sins. Let me be full of light from the Lord and make the most of every opportunity for doing good in these evil days. And let me always give thanks for everything to You my Father in the name of our Lord Jesus Christ. Amen.

In Troubling Times

One Sunday in our ladies' class, someone mentioned that she had read somewhere that most people would rather keep their own troubles than to have everyone put his or her troubles into a hat and draw out someone else's. I find this to be true for me, too. I think I'll just stick with my own problems. They're enough.

Like everyone else out there, our family has had its share of troubles. I suffer from a few ailments like IBS which is an annoying nuisance but not life-threatening, and I have high blood pressure and two leaky heart valves which means I tire easily and feel sluggish a lot. Over the past few years, we've dealt with financial problems off and on, but that's fairly common in this day and time. My teenagers have the normal troubles, too – pains and injuries from sports, too much homework with not enough time to get it done, boyfriend/girlfriend crises, and problems with their peers. In our marriage, Johnny and I have experienced the usual frictions, those day-to-day annoyances and disagreements. Of course, I'd have to say watching my mom suffer with cancer was easily the worst of my problems.

However, I would take these troubles over anyone else's any day. For instance, in no way would I want to be in the shoes of the parents who lost their young children in the school shooting in Newtown, Connecticut. Neither would I want to trade places with a friend of a friend whose daughter recently committed suicide. My heart breaks for the parents of a local three-year-old girl who is undergoing treatment for cancerous tumors, but I can't say that I would want to let my daughter take her place. Then too I do not want to be in my friend's place, as she wonders if her marriage will survive or if divorce will tear her family apart.

I think I'll just keep my list of troubles and offer them up to God in prayer. I know He will help me with the day-to-day molehills and the once-in-a-blue-moon mountains. He doesn't always take away the troubles, but He has always helped me live through them and become a better person because of them.

You should do the same: don't envy others their problems; accept the ones you've been given, but offer them up to God in prayer, believing without a doubt He will help You survive them.

In Troubling Times: Prayer

Listen to my pleading, O Lord. Be merciful and answer me! My heart has heard You say, "Come and talk with Me," and my heart responds, "Lord, I am coming." Do not hide Yourself from me. Don't leave me; don't abandon me. I will wait patiently; I will be brave and courageous. Yes, I will wait patiently for the Lord.

I trust in You Lord. I am overcome with joy because of Your unfailing love, for You have seen my troubles, and You care about the anguish of my soul. I shall rejoice in every good thing which You have given to me and my house. For every good gift and every perfect gift is from above and comes down from the Father of lights.

I will call to You whenever trouble strikes, and You will answer me. Lord, don't hold back Your tender mercies from me. My only hope is in Your unfailing love and faithfulness. For troubles surround me – too many to count! They pile up so high I can't see my way out. They are more numerous than the hairs on my head. I have lost all my courage. I am poor and needy, but You are thinking about me right now. You are my helper and my savior. Do not delay, O my God.

Though I feel like I am stumbling right now, I will not fall, for You uphold me with Your hand. Make my steps firm. I want to walk in fellowship with You, Father, and with Your son Jesus Christ. Help me to set my mind on things above, not on earthly things, for Your way is perfect. Since Your word is flawless, let it dwell in me richly.

Sometimes I feel as though disaster has overtaken me suddenly and that I can't charm it away. I feel that calamity has fallen upon me, but I can't buy my way out. Catastrophe sometimes arises so fast that I don't even know what hits me. But I do know that I can I call upon You in this day of trouble; You will deliver me, and I shall glorify You. You, who have shown me great and severe troubles, shall revive me again, and bring me up again from the depths of the earth. You shall increase my greatness, and comfort me on every side.

I will praise You – and Your faithfulness, O my God! My lips shall greatly rejoice when I sing to You, and my soul, which You have redeemed. My tongue shall talk of your righteousness all day long. I am confident I will see the Lord's goodness while I am here in the land of the living. I pray these things in Your Son's precious name. Amen.

Battling Cancer

This prayer has special meaning to me because my mom, Priscilla Phelps, passed away in 2012 from lung cancer. Her struggle with cancer began in 2008. For several weeks she dealt with a persistent pain near her left shoulder blade that she blamed on a work injury. She had spent several days moving around inventory in the parts room at the car dealership where she worked. But, when the pain didn't go away, she finally made an appointment and went to the doctor. Thinking it was nothing, she didn't tell me about this appointment. However, it wasn't nothing after all; in fact, it was definitely something, something unexpected and life-changing.

On November 7, 2008, my mom called to tell me that she had been diagnosed with lung cancer. Because she had smoked since her teens, this was not a surprise, but that didn't make it hurt any less. I felt like my world had caved in; my mom had the unspeakable "C" word. I couldn't imagine how she must have felt. Through the next three and a half years which both dragged and went by way too fast, my mom first agreed to an invasive surgery to remove half of her left lung then went on to endure three separate rounds of chemo and radiation. The chemo caused most of her long gray hair to fall out, and the radiation destroyed part of her esophagus resulting in a permanent case of laryngitis and extreme weight loss; at one time she dwindled to a mere 89 pounds. She also suffered with a constant sharp pain in her shoulder from the incision and the cancer itself, and the pain sometimes radiated across her back and under her breast.

Although this disease ravaged her body and her strength, God granted her many "good days" in which she enjoyed spending time with her husband of 43 years, her two children, and her four grandchildren. The misery of the hard days was minimized by the close relationships she had with her mother and two sisters who lived nearby and by the unexpected reconciliation with her childhood best friend, who was fighting her own battle with cancer.

Of course, I've never offered up as many prayers in my life as I did during this trying time, and I begged everyone I knew to pray, too. There were times when her health was so bad and I was so scared of losing her that all I could pray was, "Jesus, please, Jesus," over and over. The Holy Spirit had to intercede on my behalf during those times. Throughout her fight with cancer, I saw firsthand how God answered prayers, which in turn furthered my belief that prayer works and should be a major part of a Christian's daily walk with God.

My belief that God always answers prayers was confirmed every day throughout those three and a half years, but never more than those last few days of my mom's life. On March 28th of 2012, I received a call at school from my husband with a message from my aunt saying that I was to head straight to my parents' house, that my mom had less than 24 hours to live. I prayed almost nonstop during the four-hour drive home. Thankfully, my best friend Tammy volunteered to drive me there.

Needless to say, nothing could have prepared me for the sight of my mom whose body was barely lingering here. Having seen her just the week before, I was appalled at how quickly her body had deteriorated. The nurses were wrong about how long she had left; my mom didn't die the next day. She held on for five more days, passing away on April 2, 2012. Between those two dates, her family and friends gathered at her bedside, professing their love for her, sharing stories with her, and praying for her release from pain and this life. I firmly believe that it was God's will that she remained with us for those extra days because my dad was not ready to let her go. Thank God, the pain pump that had been inserted under the skin of her abdomen helped manage her pain, so she did not suffer during those last few days. God allowed each of us time to say our goodbyes and comforted us with His peace.

Cancer is a horrible, horrible disease that destroys the life of its victim and affects every member of the family. It is scary and it is deadly, but it can be defeated by God's healing hand. Know that God is stronger than any disease. Pray with a firm constitution that God will answer your prayer and heal your sick body. Be honest with Him during each stage of your treatment. Tell Him your fears; complain to Him about your pain; ask Him, why you? Being omnipotent, He's big enough to handle whatever questions you throw at Him. Don't be afraid to pray that it is His will that the cancer be eradicated from your body. Believe in what you pray. Believe in the healing power of God Just believe.

Battling Cancer: Prayer

With all my heart I praise You, O Lord my God. I will give glory to Your name forever, for so great is the love You have lavished on me, that I should be called a child of God. Yes, You have been with me from birth; from my mother's womb You have cared for me. No wonder I am always praising You!

Listen closely to my prayer; hear my urgent cry. Listen to my voice this morning, Lord. Each morning I bring my requests to You and wait expectantly. I come to You weary and burdened, and know that You will give me rest and strength and will bless me with Your peace.

How kind, how good, and how merciful You are. Now I can rest again, for You have been so good to me. You have saved me from death, my eyes from tears, my feet from stumbling. For You are great and perform great miracles. You alone are God. I walk in Your presence as I live here on this earth. My life is an example to many, because You have been my strength and protection. That is why I can never stop praising You; I declare Your glory all day long.

Turn Your ear to me; come quickly to my rescue; be my rock of refuge, a strong fortress to save me. Free me from the cancerous trap that has been set for me, for You are my refuge. Into Your hands I commit my spirit; redeem me, O God of truth. I trust in You, Lord. I will be glad and rejoice in Your love, for You see my affliction and know the anguish of my soul. You have not handed me over to the enemy but have set my feet in a spacious place.

Have mercy on me, Lord, for I am in distress. My sight is blurred because of my tears. My body and soul are withering away. I am dying from grief; my years are shortened by sadness. Misery has drained my strength. I am wasting away from within. You Lord will sustain me on my sickbed and restore me from this bed of illness. Though You have made me see troubles, many and bitter, You will restore my life again. Be merciful to me, Lord, for I am faint. O Lord, heal me, for my bones are in agony.

Because of this cancer, I am a dread to my friends—they are afraid to come near me. I am forgotten by them as though I were dead; I have become like broken pottery. Forgive them, for they do not know what their rejection does to me. Let Your unfailing love comfort me. Surround me with Your tender mercies so I might live.

I trust in You for You created my inmost being; You formed me in my mother's womb. I am marvelously made! You know me inside and out; You know every bone in my body; You know exactly how I was made, bit by bit, how I was sculpted from nothing into something. Like an open book, You watched me grow from conception to birth; all of the stages of my life were spread out before You, the days of my life all prepared before I'd lived even one day.

My future is in Your hands; deliver me from my enemy, this cancer that ravages my body. Let Your face shine on me, Your servant; save me in Your unfailing love. Let me not be put to shame for I have cried out to You. How great is Your goodness. Praise the Lord, for You have shown me Your unfailing love.

Your love and faithfulness never leave me; let me bind them around my neck and write them on the tablet of my heart. Help me to trust in You Lord with all my heart; help me in all my ways acknowledge You, fear You, and turn my back on evil. Then I will gain renewed health and vitality. I depend on You alone to save me. Through Christ's name I pray this prayer. Amen.

For Comfort

My grief is constantly shifting and changing, never staying the same for long. One minute it's a sharp pain to my chest, stealing my breath and ripping out my soul. The next it's a raw ache in my stomach, doubling me over and making me feel like I need to throw up. Soon after it's a tight pressure behind my eyes, making the tears roll down my face as I try to hold them in. But most of the time, it's a dull presence roaming about my body tapping me on my shoulder to remind me that it's there.

My grief occurs at the strangest of times. Once it found me in McDonald's in the order line behind a woman that reminded me of my grandmother. Another time it snuck up on me as I tried a new flavor of Rice-a-roni, which ironically tasted like tapioca pudding, the last food my mom was able to eat. Often it surprises me while I'm driving and slams into me from nowhere. But most often it nudges me every morning when I look in the mirror and see my mom's face in mine.

Grief is not an easy thing to handle alone. It can be all-consuming and sickening. Unfortunately, our friends and family who mean well can't take away our pain with calls, hugs, or food. They can't understand our grief because no two people grieve the same. Yet, our Father has sent us His Holy Spirit, who is our Comforter. He can take away our pain or at least dull it so we can continue on with living. If grief is crushing you today, sit on Your Father's lap, and ask Him to pour out an extra portion of His Spirit. You'll feel better, I promise.

For Comfort: Prayer

Be merciful to me, O Lord, for I am in distress; my eyes grow weak with sorrow, my soul and my body with grief. I am worn out from sobbing. Every night tears drench my bed; my pillow is wet from weeping. My vision is blurred by grief. You hear my crying; you hear my plea. You will answer my prayer.

My heart has heard You say, "Come and talk with me." And my heart responds, "Lord, I am coming." I weep with grief; encourage me by Your word. I lie in the dust, completely discouraged; I am but a shadow of my former self. Revive me by Your word. My eyes are straining to see Your promises come true. When will You comfort me?

I know Your word says that there is a time to weep and a time to laugh, a time to mourn and a time to dance. Right now, I feel like my grief is beyond healing and my heart is broken. Like Job's friends, my friends say if it were up to them, they would encourage me and take away my grief. But right now, no one is near to comfort me, to restore my spirit, or to encourage me.

Only Your unfailing love is my comfort. Being my shepherd, Your rod and Your staff comfort me. As a mother comforts a child, You will comfort me. It comforts me to know that Jesus went to Mary and Martha to comfort them when Lazarus died and that He too wept in grief. Father, shower me with Your comfort through Christ.

You keep track of all my sorrows. You have collected all my tears in Your bottle. You have recorded each one in Your book. I can't wait for the future when You will live with us and will wipe every tear from our eyes. There will be no more death or mourning or crying or pain, for the old order of things will pass away.

Lord, You hear me when I call to You for help. You rescue me from my troubles. You are close to the brokenhearted; You rescue those who are crushed in spirit. You will lift me out of this pit of despair, out of the mud and mire of mourning. You will set my feet on solid ground and steady me as I walk along from this day forth.

Turn my mourning into joyful dancing. Take away my clothes of mourning and clothe me in joy, that I might sing praises to You and not be silent. O Lord my God, I will give You thanks forever! In Jesus' name, I pray this prayer. Amen.

Dealing with Illness

You would think that in this day and time with our medical advances that sickness would be less common than it is. But, unfortunately, that's not the case. We're surrounded by illness - some deadly, some dangerous, and some just annoying and irritating.

Over the past couple of years, my family has had its share of various ailments. All four of us have had bouts with seasonal allergies and sinus infections. Being an outdoorsman, Johnny has had both Lyme's disease and Rocky Mountain spotted tick fever. Both my husband and son have lactose intolerance, and I suffer from IBS (irritable bowel syndrome). This weekend, Savanah's best friend, Ashley, stayed with us and had the stomach virus that's been going around, so probably some of us will have it by next week. Fortunately, we all seemed to have missed out on getting the whooping cough that has gone rampant through our school system this month.

We all know that God cares about us, even when we're sick. Jesus spent the last three years of His life traveling about the land healing the people of their sicknesses and diseases. He healed various ailments, from Simon's mother-in-law's fever to blood disorders to extremely contagious leprosy. He even assigned the work of healing the sick to the apostles when He sent them out on their own.

God cared then, and He still cares now. Don't lie there as though you feel you deserve this sickness you're experiencing. Don't feel you must suffer through your illness in silence. Instead, bow down and touch the fringe of Jesus' robe and ask for His healing power. Believe that He will answer, "Be encouraged! Your faith has made you well." (Matt. 9:22 NLT)

Dealing with Illness: Prayer

Give ear to my words, O Lord, consider my sighing. Listen to my cry for help, my King and my God, for I will never pray to anyone but You. In the morning, O Lord, You hear my voice; in the morning I lay my requests before You and wait in expectation. I, by Your great mercy, will come into Your house; in reverence will I bow down toward Your holy temple. Lead me, O Lord, in Your righteousness. Let me take refuge in You and be glad; let me ever sing for joy. Spread Your protection over me, that I who love Your name may rejoice in You.

I don't want to be like Asa, who even when his foot disease became life threatening did not seek Your help but sought help only from his physicians. I want You to nurse me when I am sick and ease my pain and discomfort.

Be merciful to me, O LORD, for I am in distress; my eyes grow weak with sorrow, my soul and my body with grief. My life is consumed by anguish; my strength fails because of my affliction, and my bones grow weak. But I trust in You, O Lord; I say, "You are my God." Let Your face shine on your servant; save me in Your unfailing love, for I have cried out to You. Lord, sustain me on this sickbed and restore me from this bed of illness. Heal me for my body is in agony. I am sick at heart.

I know You have seen what I do; You have seen my sins, but I pray You will heal me anyway. I pray You will lead me and comfort me, that words of praise will be on my lips. I pray You will let me have peace and that You will heal me completely. When Jesus was on this earth, He cured many people of their various diseases, and He cast out evil spirits and restored sight to the blind. I pray that You too will have compassion on me and will heal me of my affliction.

Your word claims that the earnest prayer of a righteous person has great power and wonderful results and that a prayer offered in faith will heal the sick, and You will make the person well. So, Lord, my God, I cry out to You for help, and pray that in Your compassion You will restore my health. I pray You will give me back my health and heal me my wounds. In Christ's holy name, I ask. Amen.

When You Are in a Funk

Over the years, Tammy and I have noticed that as we've gotten older, our emotions have changed. Things that once held our interest and brought us much joy and excitement no longer bring us such feelings. Instead, we're bored with our lives and could care less about things that were once important. When Tammy recently mentioned that she felt like she has been in a funk, I decided that that phrase describes how I've felt lately too. I knew that "funk" would make a great topic for a prayer. With all the stresses and hectic schedules in today's world, I think more and more women are experiencing this funk.

When I looked up the word, I discovered that "funk" is an American slang word that means depressed or upset, and it is derived from the Flemish word "fonck" which means disturbed or agitated. I was surprised at how little I could find about this word; I really thought there would be more to it than that. To me, "funk" means that apathetic, robotic, autopilot setting that so many of us function from nowadays. Sometimes that apathy slowly segues into anxious and stressful moments filled with unbelievably draining tiredness where you get what I call "fuzzy brain." Sometimes you even move on to surprising bursts of inconceivable anger or short, unexpected crying jags.

I'm not sure if this funk is common to all people or just those of us who are females over the age of forty. Either way, I'm sure there are those of you out there who are right now in a funk and don't want to be. When I was finding scriptures for this prayer, I noticed that in the psalms David often wrote about being in a funk; he just didn't use those exact words. He told God he felt like he was sinking into the mire; he was exhausted; he wept and felt everyone was out to get him; he was jealous of those who had it better than he did; he was bitter and felt that God was angry with him. But he knew the answer to being in a funk: cry out to God for help. So, that's what I want you to do, too: cry out to the One who understands your funk and will lift you up again.

When You Are in a Funk: Prayer

I trust in You at all times, so I will pour out my heart to You. O God, listen to my complaint. I am overwhelmed with longing for Your help. You know I am exhausted from crying; my throat is parched and dry. My eyes are swollen from weeping. I am waiting for You to help me. I keep right on praying to You, Lord, hoping You will show me favor. Turn Your ear to listen and set me free from this funk I am in.

Your unfailing love is better to me than life itself, so I should praise You! God, You are my God. I can't get enough of You! I've worked up such a hunger and thirst for You; it's like I've been traveling across dry and weary deserts. In your place of worship, my eyes are open; I drink in Your strength and glory. In Your generous love, I am really living at last. I want to say I bless You every time I take a breath.

Instead I don't sleep. I am too distressed even to pray! I think of the good old days, long since ended, when my nights were filled with joyful songs. I search my soul and think about the difference now. I feel so close to the edge of the cliff; my feet are slipping, and I am almost gone. I envy the proud, the healthy, the strong. It is so hard to keep my heart pure and keep myself from doing wrong. All I get is trouble all day long; every morning brings me pain. I realize how bitter I have become, how pained I have been by all I have seen. I am foolish and ignorant.

Yet I know I still belong to You; You are holding my right hand. You will keep on guiding me with Your counsel, leading me to a glorious destiny. How good it is to be near You. I will sing of Your strength, in the morning I will sing of Your love; for You are my fortress, my refuge in times of trouble. When my heart is broken, You are right there; when I feel like I've been kicked in the gut, You help me catch my breath.

When I feel as though You have been angry with me, please restore me to Your favor. When my heart is filled with sins, forgive them all. Let me live forever in Your sanctuary, safe beneath the shelter of Your wings!

There can be no joy for me until You act. Create a clean heart for me, God; put a new faithful spirit deep inside me! Please don't throw me out of Your presence; please don't take Your Holy Spirit away from me. Return the joy of Your salvation to me and sustain me with a willing spirit. When doubts fill my mind, comfort me with renewed hope and cheer.

I want to honor You as long as I live, lifting up my hands to You in prayer, and I want to praise You with songs of joy. I want to be the kind of person who lies awake thinking of You, meditating on You through the night. I will recognize how much You have helped me. I want to praise Your name with singing and honor You with thanksgiving, for this will please You more than sacrifices.

Satisfy me with Your unfailing love; give me gladness in proportion to my former misery. Replace the evil times with good. Let me see Your glory at work. Show me Your approval and make my efforts successful. Remember me and richly bless me. In Jesus' name, I pray. Amen.

Thanksgiving

I like to think that I'm a grateful person. I tend to thank God for various things throughout the day, and I try to begin every full prayer with a moment of thanksgiving. He deserves it; we'd have nothing if it weren't for Him.

Let me just share my last twenty-four hours' worth of thankful moments. When I got out of bed yesterday morning, I was thankful that the quilt I'd put on the bed under the fitted sheet seemed to help with the excess heat that the new memory foam mattress seems to exude. I was thankful, like I always am, for my extra hot shower and my quiet time before I got the kids up for school. I've been thankful lately that I haven't been missing Mama as much; I don't see her every time I look at myself in the mirror now, and I don't tear up whenever I put on her wedding ring.

During my morning prayer, I was thankful to be able to praise God for the improvements that some of the people on my daily prayer list have made. Gia's infection is leaving and her eyesight is returning; Jim's showing daily gains as he recovers from a traumatic head injury; Karen received news that the cancer is gone; and it turns out that Kay Kay only broke one bone in her shoulder and didn't crush her shoulder like they first thought.

For breakfast, I was thankful that a banana and two pieces of bacon stifled my hunger pains. I went on to school thankful that in three regular school days and two semester test days, we will be on a much-needed two-week Christmas vacation. During my prep period, I went to the bank and cashed in the change and check that was in the donation jar. Our youth group spent two Saturdays raising money for Jim (the one I mentioned above). I was grateful that God blessed Johnny and me with children who have such giving hearts. As always, I thanked God for the opening in traffic as I turned onto Highway 65.

As the day progressed, I was thankful for well-behaved students, time to grade the book assignments that they'd just turned in, and a school day that passed quickly. I thanked God that there was no after school program this week; as much as I love the money that I make from tutoring three days a week, I was ready for a small break. I enjoyed time with Brandon and his friend Caleb at McDonald's after school and enjoyed my plain double cheeseburger, fries, and Coke.

From there, I went to the basketball games and worked at the concession stand. I was thankful that I got to work on the front line serving the customers and didn't have to work in the kitchen area. Some days I really miss the fast food business, so I loved getting caught up in the rush of serving others. I also got to talk to Tammy, even though it was only for five minutes. I'm happy any time I get to spend time with her. I was also thankful that I got to watch my daughter Savanah sing the National Anthem before the senior high games and that she did so well. The bauble she made with a couple of words (and her quick apology as she did) was a big hit. I love that my girl is talented like that (I have to live vicariously through her, in that respect). I enjoyed watching the end of the senior boys' game against Stuttgart where Marcus scored the winning points in the last second of the game.

From the games, I went home, grateful to be off my feet and that it wasn't so late considering it was a game night. I talked to Johnny on the phone, glad to hear his voice and hear that he'd had a good day at work. I watched television for a few minutes with Brandon then headed off to bed and said a short prayer before I dropped right off to sleep. I'm so thankful that I don't suffer from insomnia like Johnny and so many others; I look forward to bed every night.

This morning, I was thankful that when I stepped on the scale, it revealed I had lost a pound since yesterday (one of the two that I'd gained after binging on Funyuns and home-made soup and cornbread all weekend). And I thanked God that although I have duty at school, at least it's cafeteria duty and not the dreaded mall duty (which means I'd be outside with 250 kids for fifteen minutes before school and thirty minutes at lunch).

Now that I've told you my thankful moments of my last twenty-four hours, I think it would be beneficial for you to reflect on the last day of your life, or maybe the last week, or even the last year. What all do you have to be thankful for? Do you recognize God's loving imprint on your life? Can you see how many blessings you've had? Do you thank Him for every good thing? If not, begin now; go to Him with a grateful heart. Make thanksgiving a daily part of your prayers. In all things be grateful to your Father and be sure to tell Him you recognize just how blessed you are.

Thanksgiving: Prayer

Giving thanks is a sacrifice that truly honors You. If I keep to Your path, You will reveal to me the salvation of God.

I will speak of the glorious splendor of Your majesty, and I will meditate on Your wonderful works. I will proclaim Your great deeds. I will thank You, Lord, with all my heart; I will tell of all the marvelous things You have done. Your plans for me are too numerous to list. If I tried to recite all Your wonderful deeds, I would never come to the end of them. I will be filled with joy because of You. I will sing praises to Your name, O Most High.

Praise the Lord! For You have heard my cry for mercy. You are my strength, my shield from every danger. I trust in You with all my heart. You help me, and my heart is filled with joy. I burst out in songs of thanksgiving.

You are gracious and compassionate, slow to anger and rich in love. You are good to all. You have compassion on all You have made. You uphold all who fall and lift up all who are bowed down. You open Your hand and satisfy the desires of every living thing. You are righteous in all of Your ways and loving toward all You have made. You are near to all who call on You in truth. You fulfill the desires of those who fear You; You hear their cry and save them. You watch over all who love You, but You will destroy all of the wicked. My mouth will speak in praise of You O Lord.

You heal the brokenhearted and bind up their wounds. You count the stars and call them by name. How great are You Lord! Your power is absolute! Your understanding is beyond comprehension! You support the humble and bring the wicked down to the dust. I sing out my thanks to my God. You cover the heavens with clouds, provide rain for the earth, and make the green grass grow in mountain pastures. You feed the wild animals. You bless our children, send peace across our nation, and satisfy us with plenty of food. You delight in those who honor You, those who put their hope in Your unfailing love.

You are my Master! All the good things I have are from You. I give glory to You all day long and constantly praise Your name. My life is an example to many, because You have been my strength and protection. That is why I can never stop praising You; I declare Your glory all day long.

I give thanks to You for everything. I will sing praises to You even with my dying breath. In the name of our Lord Jesus Christ. Amen.

For Guidance

Being a seventh grade English teacher, I'm constantly searching for new books for my classroom library. It now contains 2800 books, but one can never have enough books, right?! To find new books, I spend several hours each month researching books appropriate for teens on Amazon.com. I also get emails each month from teenreaders.com with suggestions of reading materials for my teens. Several teachers and I recommend and share books that we love with each other, so I find new books that way, too. To find cheaper books, I sometimes go to Book Traders in Conway, local thrift shops, yard sales, and even at my local library on their $1 shelves.

One of last year's finds at the public library was the book, Lay That Trumpet in Our Hands, *by Susan Carol McCarthy. The book sat on my shelf for several months, but I just never got around to reading it. So, when my friend Becky said she needed some book suggestions, I handed it to her to try.*

She loved the book and marked a poem that she said I "had to read." She knew I was writing this book on prayer, and she said the marked prayer was an amazing example of how we should pray. Well, I finally read the poem today, and I have to admit, I love it and think it would make a great intro to this chapter on guidance. Although I still haven't read the book (shame on me), I can tell that at this point in the book the characters have come to a time of big decisions in their lives. They are seated at the table making their plans. They synchronize their watches then bow their heads and pray…

"Lawd," Luther says, low and respectful,
"You've been watchin' over us for a long time,
From our first breath to this one.
You know our hearts, Lawd.
And, You know we have no hope
Of accomplishin' our task tonight
Without Your help.
We feel, Lawd, like old Joshua, when You took him
To the great walls of Jericho and told him
To let Your trumpets blow.
Blow those trumpets, You said,
And the great walls of Jericho will come tumblin' down.
Old Joshua b'lieved You, Lawd, and so do we.
We ask You tonight:
Lay that trumpet in our hands.
We all know our part, Lawd, and we gonna do the best we can,

But it's Mist'Warren and young Robert here
Who need Your help the most.
Guide they steps, Lawd.
Protect they path.
Show them the way to the secret hidin' place and, Lawd,
Lay that trumpet in they hands.
Give it to 'em, Lawd, then bring 'em home, safe and sound.
We thank You for the help
And for the hope that fills our hearts tonight.
We bless You for the privilege of doin' this in Your name.
And we praise You, Lawd, tonight and forever.
Amen and thank God.

Notice how they pray using scripture, how they ask for guidance, how they believe in what they are asking for, and how they praise and thank God for what He is about to do. That's what prayer is all about: laying out our requests, requests that fit within His will, along with our thanks and praise, trusting in our Father to deliver an answer in compassion and love. Do likewise; go forth and pray.

For Guidance: Prayer

Listen to my voice this morning, Lord. Each morning I bring my requests to You and wait expectantly. Because of Your unfailing love, I can enter Your house; with deepest awe I will worship at Your Temple. Pay attention to my prayer, for it comes from an honest heart.

Lord, my heart is not proud; my eyes are not haughty. I don't concern myself with matters too great or awesome for me. But I have stilled and quieted myself, just as a small child is quiet with its mother. Yes, like a small child is my soul within me. I put my hope in the Lord – now and always.

You rescue those who are humble, but You humiliate the proud. Lord, You have brought light to my life; my God, You light up my darkness. Your way is perfect. Lead me in the right path, O Lord. Tell me clearly what to do, and show me which way to turn. Grant my heart's desire and fulfill all my plans.

You made me; You created me. Now give me the sense to follow Your commands. Show me the path where I should walk, O Lord; point out the right road for me to follow. Lead me by Your truth and teach me, for You are the God who saves me. All day long I put my hope in You. Guide my steps by Your word, so I will not be overcome by any evil.

You created me anew in Christ Jesus, so that I can do the good works You planned for me long ago. So, help me to be godly, for the steps of the godly are directed by You. You delight in every detail of their lives. Though they stumble, they will not fall, for You hold them by the hand. You alone know the way I should turn. Show me where to walk, for I have come to You in prayer.

I need to fix my thoughts on what is true and honorable and right, to think about things that are excellent and worthy of praise. I will keep putting into practice all I have learned from You and heard from You, and pray Your peace will be with me.

Help me to find out what is pleasing to You. Let me make the most of every opportunity for doing good in these evil days. I don't want to act thoughtlessly. Instead I want to understand what You want me to do. I will keep working toward that day when I will finally be all that Christ Jesus saved me for and wants me to be. I want to live a pure and blameless life until Christ returns. I know You will work out Your plans for my life – for Your faithful love, O Lord, endures forever. So, it is in Jesus' name I pray. Amen.

As I Age

I'm not really sure what to say about aging. It's not something I particularly enjoy. I will say that since I turned forty (three years ago), I have noticed the aging process taking place on an almost daily basis. Like a new car depreciates in value as it leaves the lot, I feel like my body's value has depreciated in the past five years. New wrinkles are cropping up; cellulite is taking over; my eyesight is diminishing; and my hips are spreading as the scale chronicles new records of weight gain. I'd have to say "sluggish" is the word that best describes the forties. I have trouble remembering things - an elusive word during a conversation, the reason I've entered a room, an item on my to-do-list, a student's name, or the two items I needed from Wal-Mart; I spend lots of time staring at the television; and my books don't hold my attention as much as they used to. It's depressing, really.

But growing older is not all bad. I am more mature now and wiser. In a large part, I have outgrown my shyness. Over time, several of my relationships have grown closer. With twenty years of teaching under my belt, I know I'm a better teacher now than I was even a few years ago, which benefits both me and my students. I am more comfortable with who I am and like who I've become.

God makes it clear in His word that he cares about us in each stage of our lives. He is the one who formed us in the womb; we are His masterpieces. When parents brought infants and children to Jesus, He told the disciples not to turn them away because to them belongs the Kingdom of God. Many of the psalms mention God's love of youth for the young marry, have children, are like nurtured plants and carved pillars, and have total confidence in God. As Romans 5 declares: Jesus died for us even when we were sinners. If that doesn't show how much He cares for us, then I don't know what would. Then in Leviticus, He reminds us that the elderly deserve respect for they still bear fruit even in their old age.

No matter where you are on the aging spectrum, you should remember that He loves you deeply and cares about what is going on in your life. Enjoy each stage of your life here on earth and know that each stage is one step closer to eternity with Him. Hallelujah!

As I Age: Prayer

O Lord, You alone are my hope. I've trusted You, O Lord, from childhood. Yes, You have been with me from birth; from my mother's womb You have cared for me. No wonder I am always praising You! My life is an example to many, because You have been my strength and protection. That is why I can never stop praising You; I declare Your glory all day long.

And now, in my old age, don't set me aside. Don't abandon me when my strength is failing. I will keep on hoping for You to help me; I will praise You more and more. I will tell everyone about Your righteousness. All day long I will proclaim Your saving power, for I am overwhelmed by how much You have done for me. I will praise Your mighty deeds, O Sovereign Lord. I will tell everyone that You alone are just and good.

O God, You have taught me from my earliest childhood, and I have constantly told others about the wonderful things You do. Now that I am old and gray, do not abandon me, O God. Let me proclaim Your power to this new generation, Your mighty miracles to all who come after me.

The unfailing love of the Lord never ends! By His mercies I have been kept from complete destruction. Great is His faithfulness; His mercies begin afresh each day. I say to myself, "The Lord is my inheritance; therefore, I will hope in Him!"

I know that You created me and have cared for me since before I was born. You will be my God throughout my lifetime – until my hair is white with age. You made me, and You care for me. You will carry me along and save me.

Your word says that the righteous pass away and that the godly often die before their time and no one seems to care or wonder why. No one seems to understand that You are protecting them from the evil to come. The godly who die will rest in peace. For You are creating new heavens and a new earth – so wonderful that no one will even think about the old ones anymore.

I am blessed Lord because I trust in You and have made You my hope and confidence. I am like a tree planted along a riverbank, with roots that reach deep into the water. I am not bothered by the heat or worried by long months of drought. My leaves stay green, and they go right on producing delicious fruit even in my old age.

With unfailing love You have drawn me to You. You have put Your laws in my mind, and You have written them on my heart. You are my God, and I am Yours. You forgive me my wickedness and will never again remember my sins. You have removed my rebellious acts as far away from me as the east is from the west. You are a father to me, tender and compassionate. You understand how weak I am; You know I am only dust.

My days on earth are like grass; like wildflowers, we bloom and die. The wind blows, and we are gone – as though we had never been here. But Your love remains forever with those who fear You. Your salvation extends to my children and grandchildren, to those who are faithful and obey Your commandments. May You richly bless my family and me. I will praise You Lord both now and forever! Praise the Lord! In Jesus' name, I pray. Amen.

Praising God

I must admit today has not been one of my best days. It started with last night, a restless night to say the least. I'm not sure if I should blame the full moon or the zombies that my son and his buddies were watching when I went to bed. But I sure didn't sleep well.

It continued today with two crying jags and a first-rate pity party. What's really sad is the person who set off the jags and party doesn't even know the effect that her words and behavior have on me. I want a closer relationship with her, but our personalities just don't mesh. The bond that I expect to be there just doesn't seem to exist, and I don't know how to make it happen.

There are some relationships in my life that are (or were) so easy. I was extremely close to my mom, and I miss her so much. I could talk to her about pretty much anything and enjoyed telling her about my day-to-day activities when I'd call her. I really enjoyed our thirty-minute to hour-long talks. She knew the real me and accepted me and loved me for who I am. We were alike in so many ways; I always went to her when I needed advice or affirmation. Even now when I make big decisions, I think about what she would say about the choices I'm making. I still feel her love even though she's not here to say the words.

So, you're probably wondering: How does this have anything to do with praising God? Well, in the midst of my second crying bout today while I was feeling unloved, unappreciated, and unnoticed, I realized that God probably feels the same way sometimes in regards to how I treat Him. There are many times when I neglect to spend alone time with Him, when I just try to slip Him into my already busy day. Times when I dump all of my troubles on His shoulders without so much as an "I love You." Times when I expect everything from Him without giving Him anything in return. Maybe that's why He allowed me to experience this pain today...to remind me that I am selfish in my relationship with Him. I ignore Him yet expect Him to be there for me whenever I call. I take His love for granted without showing (or telling) Him how much I love Him and how much His love means to me.

So, this prayer is for Him, to let Him know that I see how much He does for me, for others, for all of mankind, even for creation. It's to let Him know that I love Him because He first loved me. I recognize His hand in my life, and I am thankful for my relationship with Him. I praise Him - first, last, and always.

Praising God: Prayer

I will praise You, my God and King, and bless Your name forever and ever. I will bless You every day, and I will praise You forever.

I love You, Lord; You are my strength. You are my fortress and my savior; You are my rock, in whom I find protection. You are my shield, the strength of my salvation, and my stronghold. I will call on the Lord, who is worthy of praise, for You save me from my enemies.

I will thank You Lord because You are just; I will sing praises to the name of the Lord most high, for the majesty of Your name fills the earth! Your glory is higher than the heavens. When I look at the night sky and see the work of Your fingers – the moon and the stars You have set in place – what are we mortals that You should think of us, mere humans that You should care for us?

You merely spoke, and the heavens were created. You breathed the word, and all the stars were born. You gave the sea its boundaries and locked the oceans in vast reservoirs. So let everyone in the world fear the Lord, and let everyone stand in awe of You. For when You spoke the world began! It appeared at Your command.

You are the one who keeps every promise forever, who gives justice to the oppressed and food to the hungry. You free prisoners and open the eyes of the blind. You lift the burdens of those bent beneath their loads. You protect foreigners, care for orphans and widows, and frustrate the plans of the wicked.

You, O Lord, reign forever, executing judgment from Your throne. You will judge the world with justice and rule the nations with fairness. You are a shelter for the oppressed, a refuge in times of trouble. Those who know Your name trust in You, for You, O Lord, have never abandoned anyone who searches for You.

You will show me the way of life, granting me the joy of Your presence and the pleasure of living with You forever. For the Lord lives! Blessed be my rock! May the God of my salvation be exalted!

I will praise You at all times. I will constantly speak Your praises. I will boast only in You; when discouraged, I will take heart. I will tell of Your greatness and exalt Your name. Praise the Lord, I tell myself. I will praise the Lord as long as I live. In Jesus' holy name, I pray. Amen.

Resolutions

Since the end of the world did not come like predicted, you now have the opportunity to make this year the best year of your life. I'm sure you've made resolutions similar to mine: to lose weight, to pray more, to be a better person, be a wiser spender, and to enjoy life more.

Did you know that all of these resolutions are possible with God? That's right. God can improve our health, draw us closer to Him, clean us up, help us financially, and give us life to the fullest. We've just got to ask and believe in His power to answer our prayers.

Resolutions: Prayer

God, You have me where You want me, with all the time in this world and the next to shower grace and kindness on me in Christ Jesus. Saving me was all Your idea and all Your work.

So, here's what I think: The best thing I can do right now is to finish what I started last year and not let my good intentions grow stale. My heart is in the right place, and I've got what it takes to finish it. I need to roll up my sleeves and put my mind into gear. I do not want to slip lazily back into those old grooves of evil, doing just what I feel like doing. Let me be pulled into a way of life shaped by God's life, a life energetic and blazing with holiness.

Remind me today, God, that everything I have and everything I am is a gift from You. I already have all that I need. I already have more access to You than I can handle. Your Holy Spirit is moving and breathing in me, and You are the most intimate part of my life as You make me fit for You. Don't let me take such a gift for granted. I want to love You God with my whole heart, with all that's in me, with all I've got. God, rewrite the text of my life as I open my heart to Your eyes.

God, give me work to do and give me the energy to do it. Let me quietly go about my business of living simply, in humble contemplation. Let me be agreeable, be sympathetic, be loving, be compassionate, be humble. Let me bless; that's my job, to bless. I'll be a blessing and also get a blessing. I want to embrace life and see the day fill up with good.

I want to know Christ personally, experience His resurrection power, be a partner in His suffering, and go all the way with Him to death. I am a citizen of heaven, waiting for the arrival of the Savior, who will transform our earthly bodies into glorious bodies like His own. It is in my Savior's blessed name that I pray. Amen.

Endnote

I have found that writing a book is thrilling, time-consuming, and draining, but I am so thankful that God planted the idea of this book into my mind. The researcher in me has had so much fun digging through various translations of the Bible to find the right words for each prayer. As for the introductions to each chapter, I never knew I had so much to say about my life.

I pray that you, the reader, have found several prayers that you've been able to use in your one-on-one time with God. I pray that you have seen the benefits of using scriptures in your talks with God. I pray in the future you will venture forth and create your own scriptural prayers, ones that are more personal than these could be. But most importantly, I pray that you will wake up each day with an intense longing to draw closer to God through Jesus Christ our Savior, no matter what it takes. God bless you!

Verses Used in Prayers

Key:

> NLT – New Living Translation
> NIV – New International Version
> MSG – The Message
> GW – God's Word
> NKJ – New King James

Forgive My Sins:
NLT – Psalms 19:12-14; 25:7, 11; 28:6-7; 32:3-5; 39:1; 51:1-2, 7, 17; 69:5-6; 2 Cor. 7:9-10
NIV – Psalm 41:4; Rom. 7:15, 17
MSG – Psalm 51:4-6, 16
NKJ – Is. 1:18

Salvation:
NLT – Eph. 1:4-5
NIV – John 16:1; Acts 2:38; 3:19; 4:12; 22:16; Rom. 3:22-23; 6:304; 2 Cor. 3:18; 5:9-10, 21; Eph. 2:10; Phil. 1:6, 9-10; Col. 1:10-12

Relieve My Fears:
NLT – Psalms 1:3, 6; 3:5; 16:7-8; 23:4; 27:14; 31:2; 34:4,7; 91:5-6, 9-11, 14-16; Is. 43:1-3, 10-11; Jer. 46:28

Looking for a Spouse:
NIV – Psalms 6:9, 37:7; 38:8; 51:10; 69:20; 86:11-12; 139:5; Jer. 29:11; Rom. 12:1; Acts. 1:2:42; 1 Cor. 6:13; Eph. 5:3; Col. 3:12-14

To Be a Better Wife:
NLT – Job 8:7; Psalms 4:6; 37:4; Prov. 16:3; SoS 1:9, 15: 6:3; 8:6, 10; Matt. 6:28; 1 Cor. 7:4; 13:4-7; Gal. 6:2; Eph. 4:26; 5:22; 1 Pet. 3:4, 7
NIV – Phil. 4:12-13
MSG – SoS – 1:1; 6:4, 8; 1 Pet. 3:1, 3-4

We Want a Baby:
NIV – Deut. 30:9; 1 Sam. 1:20; Job 30:16; Psalms 4:1; 5:3; 20:4; 31:19; 37:7; 38:8; 57:7; 62:1; 69:13; 86:1, 11-12; 119:58, 116; 127:3; 139:5; 143:1; Dan. 9:17; Gal. 5:5

During Pregnancy:

NLT – Psalms 115:14; 127:3; 147:13; Eccl. 11:5
NIV – 1 Sam. 1:10; Psalms 6:2; 28:1; 30:11; 39:12; 119:147-148; 139:13-16; Prov. 3:8; Eccl. 9:7; Jer. 1:12; Matt. 9:20; Heb. 4:12

For a Working Mother:
NLT – Psalms 5:1-2; 18:30; Eccl. 5:20; Is. 41:10; Col. 3:13-15; 1 Thes. 5:11; 1 John 1:3
NIV – Deut. 11:13, 19; Psalms 5:1, 3; 18:28-29; 37:4; 128:2; Prov. 31:11-12, 17, 20, 23, 25-28; Eccl. 5:18-19; Matt. 11:28; Gal. 6:9; Col. 3:2, 12; 1 Thes. 5:16-18, 23; 1 John 3:1, 18

Safety:
NIV – Ex. 13:21; 34:9; Psalms 4:8; 12:7; 16:1; 18:35; 31:19; 32:7; 91:11; 140:4; Prov. 29:25; 30:5; Ezra 8:21; 1 Tim. 4:18; Jude 1:1
MSG – Psalms 34:7, 20; 37:39-40; 62:2, 7-8; 91:3, 9; 121:5-8
GW – Is. 32:18

Daily Worries:
NLT – 1 Sam. 1:15; Psalms 23:1-3, 5-6; Matt. 6:34; Phil. 4:6-7; 1 Tim. 6:9-10, 21; James 4:13-16
NIV – Psalm 62:1-2; Is. 26:4; Jer. 29:11; Rom. 12:2, Col. 3:17; Heb. 4:12, 1 Thes. 4:11

Friendship:
NLT – Psalm 15:2-3; Prov. 12:26; Matt. 7:5; 1 Cor. 1:4, 8-9; 13:5; Eph. 4:2, Col. 1:10; 3:14, 4:2
NIV – Psalm 41:9; Prov. 17:17; Matt. 7:12; Gal. 6:4-5; Col. 3:12, 15; Heb. 10:24-25; 1 Thes. 4:18, 1 John 3:18
MSG – James 5:16
ESV – 2 Thes. 3:13

Let Me Forgive:
NLT - Psalms 26:2, 86:11; Prov. 29:22; Is. 55:11; Rom. 12:2, 19-20; Eph. 4:2; 5:2, 8, 16, 20; Col. 3:8, 13
NIV – Psalms 26:2; 86:11; Prov. 19:11; 22:24-25; Matt. 5:23; 6:14; 18:22; Mark 11:25; Acts 4:29; Eph. 4:26; Col. 3:12

In Troubling Times:
NLT – Psalms 27:7-9, 13-14; 31:6-7; 40:11-12, 17; 86:7; Is. 47:11
NIV – Psalms 18:30; 37:23-24; Col. 3:2, 16
NKJ – Deut. 26:11; Psalms 50:15; 71:20-24; James 1:17

Battling Cancer:
NLT – Psalms 5:3; 31:9-12, 14-15; 33:20; 71:6-8; 86: 6, 10, 12-13; 116:5-9; 119:76-77; 139:16; Prov. 3:8; Matt. 11:28
NIV – Psalms 31:1-5, 7-8; Prov. 3:3, 5-7; 1 John 3:1
MSG – Psalm 139:13-15

For Comfort:
NLT – Job 16:5; 17:7; Psalms 6:6-7; 24:1; 27:8; 30:11-12; 34:17-18; 40:2; 56:8; 119:25, 28, 82; Jer. 8:18
NIV – Psalms 23:4; 31:9; 119:76; Eccl. 3:4; Is. 66:13; Lam. 1:16; John 11:19; 2 Cor. 1:5; Rev. 21:3-4

Dealing with Illness:
NLT – 2 Chron. 16:12; Psalms 30:2; 41:3; Is. 57:18-19; Jer. 30:17; Luke 7:21; James 5:15-16
NIV – Psalms 5:1-3, 7-8, 11-12; 6:3; 31:9-10, 14, 16

When You Are in a Funk:
NLT – Psalms 61:4; 65:3; 69:3, 13, 30-31; 71:2-6; 90:14-16, 19; 116:12
NIV – Psalms 59:16, 60:1, 62:8
MSG – Psalms 34:18, 63:1, 63:2, 4

Thanksgiving:
NLT – Psalms 9:1; 16:2; 28:6-7; 40:5; 44:8; 50:23; 71:7; 146:2; 147:3-6, 8-9, 11, 13-14
NIV – Psalm 145:5-6, 8-9, 14, 16-21

For Guidance:
NLT – Psalms 17:1; 18:27-28, 30; 20:4, 25:4-5; 119:73, 133; 131:1-3; 138:8; 142:3; 143:8; Eph. 2:10; 5:10, 16-17; Phil. 1:10; 3:12

As I Age:
NLT – Psalms 71:5-9, 14-18; 103:12-19; 115:14, 18; Is. 46:3-4; 57:1-2; 65:17; Jer. 17:7-8; Lam. 3:22-24

Praise God:
NLT – Psalms 7:17; 8:3; 9:7-10; 16:11; 18:1-3, 46; 33:6-9; 34:1-3; 113:4; 144:3; 145:1-3; 146:1-2, 6-10; 148:13

Resolutions:
MSG - Deut. 6:5; 2 Sam. 22:25; 1 Cor. 4:6-7, 15:11; 2 Cor. 8:10-11; Eph. 2:7-8; Phil. 3:10, 20-21; 1 Peter 1:13-16, 3:8-10; 1 Tim. 2:3

Bibliography

McCarthy, Susan Carol. *Lay That Trumpet in Our Hands*. New York: Bantam, 2002. Print.

About the Author

Kim Trujillo is happily married and has two teenage children, a son and a daughter. She has been a teacher for twenty years and currently teaches English language arts to seventh graders in a small town in Arkansas. She leads the ladies' class at her church on Sundays as well.

She is an avid reader and verges on being a reading addict. She carries a book or her Kindle with her to all school functions and local fast food restaurants.

This is Kim's first book, but she plans to add more scriptural prayer books to her *A Closer Talk with God* series soon. She is currently working on another series of books called *What Should I Read Next?* for teen readers.

You can contact Kim through her Facebook account, kimtrujillobooks, or her email, kimtrujillobooks@gmail.com.

Made in the USA
Lexington, KY
24 May 2017